What Can You See?

by Ellen Dalton

A tool can help you see.
You can read about
your world.

A tool can help you see.
You can see things
up close.

A tool can help you see.
You can see tiny things.

A tool can help you see.
You can see far.

A tool can help you see.
You can take a picture.

A tool can help you see.
You can see the sky.

Pick up a tool.
Look around your world!

What Do You See?

Pretend you are using one of the tools in the book. Tell your partner what you see.

How Tools Help

Draw a picture of someone using a tool from the book. Write about your picture.

You can see _____.

Tools We Use

GR C • Benchmark 4 • Lexile 90

Grade K • Unit 2 Week 1

www.mheonline.com

The **McGraw·Hill** Companies

ISBN-13 978-0-02-119430-8
MHID 0-02-119430-0

EAN

9 780021 194308

99701

K